SIMPLE
NEW ENGLAND
COOKERY

COMPILED BY EDNA BEILENSON

AND DECORATED BY

RUTH McCREA

Peter Pauper Press

MOUNT VERNON · NEW YORK

A Song to New England

I sing of New England
Its pumpkin and maize,
The apple pies baking
On long winter days;

The turkey a-roasting
All golden and brown,
With good apple cider
To wash the bird down!

The Indian Pudding
And Blueberry Muffin,
The thyme and the sage
In the savory stuffin',

I sing of the elm-trees
In the cool of whose shade
The pleasantest lunches
Of seafood are made!

I sing of New England,
I sing of its food!
It's hearty and tasty,
It's simple; it's good!

THE EDITOR

Soups and Chowders

Cream of Lobster Soup

2 pounds lobster
2 cups chicken stock
1/4 cup butter
1/4 cup flour
4 cups milk
1 1/2 teaspoons salt
Few grains cayenne
1/2 cup sweet cream

Remove meat from lobster shell. Add stock to body bones and tough ends of claws, cut in pieces; bring slowly to boiling point and cook 20 minutes. Drain, reserve liquor, and thicken with butter and flour cooked together.

Scald milk with tail meat of lobster, finely chopped. Strain, add to liquor. Season with salt and cayenne, and add cream. Add claw meat, and body meat, diced.

5

Lobster Chowder

2-pound boiled lobster
2 tablespoons butter
1/4 cup cracker crumbs
4 cups milk
1 slice onion
1 cup cold water
Salt and pepper to taste
Sherry, if desired

Remove meat from lobster shell and dice. Cream 2 tablespoons butter, add cracker crumbs, scald milk with onion, remove onion, and add milk to mixture.

Break up body bones and cook 10 minutes in 1 cup cold water. Strain and add to mixture with diced lobster. Season with salt and pepper. Add Sherry to taste. Serves 8.

New England Clam Chowder

3/4 cup butter
6 small onions, minced
2 pints clams, chopped
4 cups boiling water
4 potatoes, diced
Salt and pepper to taste
2 quarts milk

Melt the butter and fry onions until golden brown. Add the chopped clams and simmer 5 or 6 minutes. Add boiling water, potatoes, salt and pepper and cook for 30 minutes. Pour in milk, heat it all thoroughly; serve with oysterettes. Serves 8.

Cream of Oyster Soup

1 quart oysters
⅓ cup butter
⅓ cup flour
4 cups milk
1 slice onion
4 stalks celery, chopped
Mace
Sprig of parsley
Bay leaf
½ cup sweet cream
Salt and pepper

Clean oysters, removing bits of shell. Reserve liquor, add oysters slightly chopped, heat slowly to boiling point, and simmer 20 minutes. Strain, re-heat liquor, and thicken with butter and flour cooked together.

Scald milk with onion, celery, mace, parsley, and bay leaf; remove seasonings and add milk to oyster liquor. Add cream. Season with salt and pepper. Serves 8.

Potato Soup

8 medium-size white potatoes
2 large onions
2 stalks celery
1 carrot
Salt and pepper
Parsley, chopped
1 cup sour cream

Boil all the vegetables together in salted water. When the potatoes are soft and while the liquid is still hot force the entire mixture through a colander. Season to taste. Just before serving, add some chopped parsley and 1 cupful of sour cream.

Corn Soup

2 cups canned corn
2 cups boiling water
2 cups milk
1 slice onion
2 tablespoons butter
2 tablespoons flour
Salt and pepper

To the corn, add water, milk and onion, and cook 20 minutes in top of double boiler. Rub through sieve. Bind with butter and flour cooked together. Garnish with popped corn if desired.

Fish and Sea Food

Salmon Mold

2 cups cooked salmon
½ tablespoon salt
1½ tablespoons sugar
½ tablespoon flour
1 teaspoon mustard
¼ teaspoon pepper
2 egg yolks
2 tablespoons melted butter
¾ cup milk
¼ cup vinegar
¾ tablespoon gelatin, soaked in
    2 tablespoons cold water

Cook salmon, rinse thoroughly with hot water, and flake. Mix dry ingredients, add egg yolks, butter, milk, and vinegar. Cook over boiling water, stirring constantly until mixture thickens. Add soaked gelatin. Strain and add to salmon. Fill mold, chill, and serve with cucumber or lemon sauce. Serves 6.

Fish Salad

2 cups flaked fish
    (salmon, halibut, etc.)
½ cup mayonnaise or salad dressing
½ cup celery, diced
½ cup peas
2 tablespoons sweet pickle, chopped
2 tablespoons onion, chopped
3 hard-boiled eggs, diced
Lettuce

Combine all ingredients except the lettuce, being careful not to break the fish into too small pieces.

Serve on lettuce cups, and garnish with sliced eggs. Serves 6.

Lobster Salad

1 pound cooked lobster meat
⅓ cup mayonnaise or salad dressing
1 tablespoon lemon juice
¼ teaspoon salt
Lettuce
3 tomatoes

Cut lobster meat into ½-inch pieces. Add mayonnaise, lemon juice, and salt. Serve on lettuce, garnish with tomato wedges. Serves 6.

Lobster Mousse

½ pound cooked lobster meat
1 tablespoon gelatin, unflavored
¼ cup cold water
½ cup boiling water
½ cup celery, chopped
2 tablespoons stuffed olives, sliced
1 tablespoon onion, grated
1 teaspoon prepared mustard
½ teaspoon salt
½ cup whipping cream
¼ cup mayonnaise or salad dressing
Salad greens

Cut lobster meat into ½-inch pieces. Soften gelatin in cold water for 5 minutes. Add boiling water and stir until dissolved. Add the next 5 ingredients. Chill until almost congealed. Add lobster meat. Whip cream. Combine mayonnaise and whipped cream; fold into gelatin mixture. Place in a 1-quart mold; chill until firm. Unmold on salad greens. Serves 6.

Boiled Lobsters

2 live lobsters (1 pound each)
3 quarts boiling water
3 tablespoons salt
Melted butter
Plunge the lobsters headfirst into boiling

salted water. Cover and return to boiling point. Simmer for 20 minutes. Drain. Place lobster on its back. With a sharp knife cut in half lengthwise. Remove the stomach, which is just back of the head, and the intestinal vein, which runs from the stomach to the tip of the tail. Do not discard the green liver and coral roe; they are delicious. Crack claws. Serve with butter. Serves 2.

Lobster Stuffed Eggs

1 pound cooked lobster meat
1 teaspoon onion, grated
1 teaspoon green pepper, chopped
1 teaspoon pimiento, chopped
1 tablespoon chili sauce
⅔ cup mayonnaise
  or salad dressing
1½ dozen eggs, hard-boiled
Parsley

Chop lobster meat. Add onion, green pepper, pimiento, chili sauce, and mayonnaise. Chill. Cut eggs in half lengthwise and remove yolks. Place lobster mixture in egg whites. Garnish with parsley. Makes 36 canapés.

Codfish Balls

1 cup salt codfish
2½ cups potatoes, diced
½ tablespoon butter
1 egg, well beaten
⅛ teaspoon pepper

Wash fish in cold water and cut in small pieces. Wash and pare potatoes, dicing before measuring. Cook fish and potatoes in boiling water to cover until potatoes are nearly soft. Drain thoroughly, return to kettle in which they were cooked. Mash thoroughly, add butter, egg, and pepper. Beat with fork 2 minutes. Add salt if necessary.

Take up by spoonsful, sauté in butter or fry 1 minute in deep fat; drain on brown paper. Serves 6.

Scalloped Oysters

1 pint oysters
2 cups cracker crumbs
½ teaspoon salt
⅛ teaspoon pepper
½ cup melted butter
¼ teaspoon Worcestershire sauce
1 cup milk

Drain oysters. Combine cracker crumbs,

salt, pepper, and butter; sprinkle ⅓ in a buttered casserole, cover with a layer of oysters. Repeat layer. Add Worcestershire sauce to milk, and pour over contents of dish. Sprinkle remaining crumbs over top. Bake in 350° oven for 30 minutes or until brown. Serves 6.

Fried Oysters

1 quart oysters
2 eggs
2 tablespoons milk
1 teaspoon salt
⅛ teaspoon pepper
1 cup bread crumbs, cracker crumbs,
  or cornmeal

Drain oysters. Mix eggs, milk, and seasonings. Dip oysters in egg mixture and roll in crumbs. Fry in hot fat; when brown on one side turn and brown other side. Cooking time about 5 minutes. Drain on absorbent paper. Serve immediately with slices of lemon or tartar sauce. Serves 6.

Tartar Sauce

½ cup mayonnaise
1 Tbsp. each: onions, pickles, parsley, olives

Mix thoroughly and chill.

Oyster Fritters

1 pint oysters
2 cups sifted flour
1 tablespoon baking powder
1 1/2 teaspoons salt
2 eggs, beaten
1 cup milk
1 tablespoon melted fat

Drain oysters, and chop. Sift dry ingredients together. Combine beaten eggs, milk and fat. Pour into dry ingredients and stir until smooth. Add oysters. Drop batter by teaspoonsful into hot fat, heated to 350° and fry about 3 minutes or until golden brown. Drain on absorbent paper. Serves 6.

Sea Song Pies

1 pound salt dried codfish
3 cups water
1 cup raw potatoes, diced
1/4 cup onion, chopped
3 tablespoons butter
3 tablespoons flour
2 cups milk
Salt and pepper
Pie crust

Bring codfish to a boil in a kettle of water

18

to freshen it. Discard water, and boil fish
15 minutes in 3 cups fresh water to which
have been added diced raw potatoes and
chopped onion. Drain.

Melt butter in double boiler, and mix in
flour. Add milk gradually, stirring constantly. Cook 3 minutes, season, and add
fish and potatoes.

Divide mixture into 6 small pot pie dishes,
cover with pie crust and bake until golden
brown. Serves 6.

Oyster Stuffing

½ cup celery, chopped
½ cup onion, chopped
¼ cup butter
6 cups dry bread crumbs
1 tablespoon parsley, chopped
3 cups oysters, chopped
Salt and pepper
1 teaspoon poultry seasoning
2 eggs, beaten
1¾ cups milk and oyster liquor

Cook celery and onion in butter until
golden brown. Add crumbs and parsley;
mix thoroughly. Add oysters, seasonings,
and eggs. Add enough liquid to moisten.

Meat and Poultry

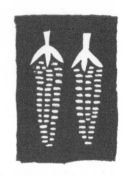

Roast Turkey

Dress and clean turkey. Rub inside with salt and pepper. Stuff neck cavity. Fasten opening with metal pins. Fill body cavity loosely with stuffing. Rub with butter or make paste of ½ cup butter, ¾ cup flour; spread over all parts of turkey.

Place turkey breast side down in open roasting pan to allow juices to run down into breast. Drip pan from broiler may be used if large roaster is not available. Roast uncovered in 300° to 325° oven 15 to 20 minutes per pound, turning turkey over onto back when half done.

Baste at 30-minute intervals with mixture of melted butter and hot water. When breast and legs become light brown, cover with brown paper. Turkey is done when the meat pulls away from the leg-bones.

Corn Bread Stuffing

1 small onion, chopped
2 tablespoons celery, chopped
¼ cup butter
Few sprigs parsley, chopped
2 cups corn bread crumbs
½ teaspoon poultry seasoning
Dash thyme
Salt and pepper

Cook onion and celery in the butter until lightly browned. Add remaining ingredients. Use as stuffing for fish. Makes about 2 cups.

Chestnut Stuffing

1 cup butter
1 cup onion, minced
1 teaspoon each thyme and sage
1½ teaspoons salt
¾ teaspoon pepper
⅓ cup parsley, chopped
¾ cup celery and leaves, chopped
2 quarts soft stale bread crumbs or cubes
1 pound Italian chestnuts, cooked,
  shelled and chopped

Melt butter in skillet, and add all ingredients, except last 2. Cook 5 minutes. Add crumbs and chestnuts. Use as stuffing for turkey. Makes about 10 cups.

Bread Crumb Stuffing

4 cups dry bread crumbs
1 medium-size onion, chopped
1 teaspoon salt
¼ teaspoon pepper
Sage to taste
Parsley, chopped
¼ teaspoon poultry seasoning
⅓ cup melted butter
Hot water or stock to moisten

Combine bread, onion, and seasoning; add butter and sufficient liquid to moisten. Mix gently. Allow 1 cup stuffing for each pound of poultry or game.

Herb Stuffing

1 medium onion, minced
2 tablespoons parsley, minced
2 tablespoons butter
2 cups soft stale bread crumbs
¼ teaspoon each thyme, marjoram,
  and rosemary
Salt and pepper to taste

Mix all ingredients, and moisten with a little water or stock. Use as stuffing for boneless pork chops. Makes about 2 cups. To prepare stuffed pork chops: put 2 thin chops together with stuffing and hold them in place with string.

Country Fried Chicken

1 frying chicken
1 teaspoon white pepper
2 teaspoons salt
3 eggs
1/4 cup milk
3/4 cup flour
2 cups cracker meal

Wash, split and cut the chicken for frying. Season with salt and pepper. Make mixture of eggs, milk and 1/2 teaspoon of salt. Pour the egg mixture over the chicken and let it stand about an hour or two. Roll chicken in flour and cracker meal which have been mixed together. Fry in medium hot fat from 12 to 15 minutes. Serves 4-5.

Brown Gravy

3 tablespoons butter
1 slice onion
4 tablespoons flour
1 1/4 cups stock or water
Salt and pepper

Fry onion in butter until slightly browned; remove onion from butter, add flour mixed with seasonings, and brown the butter and flour together. Add stock gradually, bring to boil and boil 2 minutes.

Standing Rib Roast

Select a 2- or 3-rib standing rib roast (4 to 5 pounds). Place fat side up in roasting pan; season with salt and pepper and place in 350° oven. Do not cover and do not add water.

Allow 18 to 20 minutes per pound for rare roast, 22 to 25 minutes per pound for medium, and 27 to 30 minutes per pound for well-done roasts. Serve with Yorkshire Pudding.

Yorkshire Pudding

1½ cups flour
½ teaspoon salt
1½ cups milk
3 eggs

Mix salt and flour and add milk gradually, to form paste; then add eggs and beat 2 minutes with an egg beater.

Cover bottom of 2 hot pans with melted butter; pour mixture in pan ½ inch deep.

Put in 450° oven and bake 20 to 30 minutes, decreasing the heat as the baking is accomplished. Cut in squares for serving.

Lamb Stew

3 pounds lamb, cut in pieces
½ cup carrots, diced
½ cup turnips, diced
1 celery stalk, diced
1 onion, sliced
4 cups potatoes, cut in ½-inch cubes
¼ cup flour
Salt
Pepper

Place meat in kettle, cover with boiling water, and cook slowly 2 hours or until tender. After cooking 1 hour add carrots, turnips, celery, and onions. Half an hour before serving add potatoes. Thicken with flour, mixed with ¼ cup cold water. Season with salt and pepper. Serve with dumplings. Serves 8.

New England Boiled Dinner

4 pounds corned beef, brisket preferred
8 small white onions
8 parsnips
8 carrots
8 potatoes
1 cabbage

Wash beef under running water to remove brine. Place in large kettle, cover with water, bring slowly to a boil and cook 5 minutes. Remove scum, cover and simmer 2½ hours.

Skim excess fat off liquid, then bring meat to a rolling boil; add whole onions, parsnips, carrots and potatoes, and cook gently, uncovered, 20 minutes. Then add cabbage, which has been cored and cut in eighths, and cook 20 minutes longer, or until vegetables are just tender.

Place meat on hot large platter and arrange vegetables around it. Garnish with parsley. Serves 8.

Cinnamon Apples

8 apples
8 cloves
1¼ cups sugar
2 cups water
2 cinnamon sticks

Core and pare apples. Stick with cloves. Cook sugar, water, and cinnamon five minutes. Add apples and cook very slowly until tender, basting often with syrup in pan. Serve with meat or fowl, as a garnish. Serves 8.

Vegetables and Salads

Boston Baked Beans

1 one-pound package beans
 (pea, marrow or navy)
1 medium onion
½ pound salt pork
4 tablespoons brown sugar
½ teaspoon salt
Dash pepper
1 tablespoon ketchup
1 teaspoon dry mustard
½ cup molasses
Boiling water

Wash beans, then cover with cold water and let soak overnight. In the morning, drain off the water and set beans aside. Quarter the onion and place in the bottom of bean crock; then cut the salt pork into chunks and place 3 or 4 pieces on top of the onion. Pour beans into the crock, place the rest of the salt pork on top, and sprinkle on sugar, salt, pepper, ketchup, and mustard. Finally add the molasses. Then add enough boiling water to just cover the beans.

Cover and bake in a 325° oven from 5 to 6 hours or until beans are tender and brown. Keep beans covered with liquid except during the last hour of baking when the water is allowed to bake away. About 30 minutes before the beans are done, take off the cover. Serve with brown bread. (See page 36.) Serves 6.

Scalloped Potatoes

8 medium-size potatoes, sliced
1/4 cup onion, minced
Flour for dredging
1 tablespoon butter
Salt and pepper
1 can condensed cream of mushroom soup
1 cup milk

Alternate layers of potatoes and onions in greased baking dish. Dredge with flour, dot with butter, and season each layer with salt and pepper. Mix mushroom soup and milk; pour over potatoes. Cover and bake in 350° oven 1 1/4 hours. Serves 8.

Hashed Brown Potatoes

3 cups raw potatoes, diced
6 tablespoons butter
Salt and pepper

In a heavy skillet, melt butter, then add potatoes and seasonings. Cook until tender. Stir and lift from bottom, so that the potatoes will not stick. Add more butter as needed. When brown on bottom, turn out onto serving dish. Serves 6.

Corn Fritters

1 ¾ cups sifted flour
2 teaspoons baking powder
¾ teaspoon salt
1 egg, beaten
¾ cup milk
1 cup corn kernels, drained
1 tablespoon melted butter

Sift flour, baking powder, and salt together. Combine egg, milk, corn, and butter; stir into flour mixture.

Melt shortening to ½ inch depth in frying pan. Drop batter from tip of large spoon into hot fat and fry 4 to 5 minutes, or until golden brown, turning when brown on one side; drain on brown paper. Makes about 8 fritters.

Corn Oysters

2 cups corn kernels
2 eggs, well beaten
2 tablespoons butter
1 cup flour
1 teaspoon salt
⅛ teaspoon pepper

Drain corn thoroughly, add other ingredients. Drop by spoonsful and fry in deep hot fat. The croquettes should be the size of large oysters. Drain on absorbent paper. Serves 6. Raw, cooked, or canned corn may be used.

Glazed Turnips or Parsnips

6 small turnips or parsnips
3 tablespoons melted butter
¾ cup brown stock
¼ teaspoon salt
1 teaspoon sugar
Mace

Wash, peel or scrape vegetable; cut in large cubes. Boil 5 minutes in water to cover; drain. Add turnip to remaining ingredients in heavy saucepan; bring to a boil and simmer, covered, about 20 minutes, or until tender. Uncover and cook until sauce is reduced to a glaze. Serves 4.

Coleslaw

2 to 3 cups cabbage, shredded
Salt, paprika, garlic
Sour cream dressing,
    diluted with milk or cream

Rub bowl with garlic for flavor before mixing salad in it. Pour dressing over cabbage and toss together lightly. Season to taste. Serves 6.

Sour Cream Dressing:

½ cup sour cream
2 tablespoons sugar
¼ teaspoon salt
⅛ teaspoon celery salt
Paprika
2 tablespoons vinegar

Add seasonings to cream and mix well. Stir in vinegar gradually. Makes about ⅔ cup dressing.

Fried Tomatoes

4 large tomatoes
Bread crumbs
Salt and pepper
1 egg

Wash and cut tomatoes in slices about ½ inch thick. Season the bread crumbs with the salt and pepper. Dip the tomatoes in well-beaten egg and then in the crumbs. Fry in hot shortening until golden brown. Serves 6.

Candied Carrots

2 bunches carrots
1 cup sugar
1/2 teaspoon nutmeg
2 cups water
4 slices lemon

Wash and scrape carrots, cut lengthwise. Place in saucepan with sugar, water, nutmeg and lemon and let cook for 15 to 20 minutes on a low flame, until carrots are tender and glazed. Serves 6.

Harvard Beets

2 tablespoons butter
1 tablespoon cornstarch
1 tablespoon sugar
1/4 teaspoon salt
1/4 cup vinegar
1/4 cup water
2 cups beets, cooked and cubed

Melt butter; add cornstarch, sugar, and salt; blend. Add vinegar and water; cook until thick. Pour over beets. Serves 4.

Hot Breads
and Rolls

Boston Brown Bread

1 cup flour
1 cup corn meal
1 cup coarse wheat flour
¾ tablespoon soda
1 teaspoon salt
¾ cup molasses
2 cups sour milk
  or 1¾ cups sweet milk
1 cup seedless raisins

Mix and sift dry ingredients, add molasses, milk and raisins, stir until well mixed, and fill well-greased mold not more than ⅔ full. Cover closely and place mold on trivet in kettle containing boiling water, allowing water to come half way up around mold. Cover closely and steam 3½ hours, keeping water at boiling point. Add more boiling water as needed.

In steamed pudding molds, steam 1½ to

2 hours. Take from water, remove cover, and set in 300° oven 15 minutes to dry off. Remove from molds. Cut with string while hot, by drawing string around bread, crossing, and pulling ends. Makes 2 loaves.

Note: Boston Brown Bread may be steamed in a double boiler. Grease top part and fill half full of batter. Set over lower part into which ½ inch boiling water has been poured. Cover tightly and steam 3 hours over low heat, keeping water at boiling point.

Corn Bread

1 cup corn meal
1 cup flour
3 teaspoons baking powder
½ teaspoon salt
1 egg
1 cup milk
¼ cup melted butter

Sift together corn meal, flour, baking powder and salt. Beat egg; add milk and butter. Add to dry ingredients, stirring just enough to moisten. Pour into greased pan 8 inches by 8 inches by 2 inches. Bake in 400° oven 30 minutes.

Popovers

1 cup sifted flour
1/4 teaspoon salt
3/4 cup plus 2 tablespoons milk
2 eggs
1/2 teaspoon melted shortening

Sift flour and salt. Add milk gradually to make a smooth batter. Beat eggs until light and add eggs to batter mixture. Add shortening. Beat 2 minutes with beater. Fill greased muffin pans 2/3 full. Place in 450° oven. Bake 30 minutes. Lower heat to 350° and bake 10 minutes longer.

Muffins

1/4 cup shortening
1/3 cup sugar
2 eggs, beaten
2 cups flour
3 teaspoons baking powder
1 teaspoon salt
2/3 cup milk

Cream together shortening and sugar. Add beaten eggs. Sift together flour, baking powder and salt; add alternately with milk to creamed mixture. Fill greased muffin pans 2/3 full. Bake in 400° oven 25 minutes. Makes 12.

Jiffy Oatmeal Bread

½ cup dry oatmeal
1 tablespoon brown sugar
¾ tablespoon salt
3 cups flour
1 tablespoon shortening
1 package dry yeast
½ cup lukewarm water
1¼ cups lukewarm milk

Mix dry ingredients and chop shortening into mixture with pie blender. Dissolve 1 package of dry yeast in ½ cup lukewarm water. Add this and 1¼ cups lukewarm milk to the dry mixture. Stir well, and beat by hand for 2 minutes.

Place in greased bread pan (dough will half fill a standard pan) and let rise until double in bulk.

To make dough rise quickly, cover pan with towel and place on top of warm oven. Bake at 400° for 40 to 45 minutes.

Add cinnamon and raisins to above recipe, bake in a square pan and top with a mixture of sugar, cinnamon, flour and butter, for an excellent variation of coffee cake.

Johnny Cake

1 cup sweet milk
1 cup buttermilk
1 teaspoon salt
1 teaspoon soda
1 tablespoon melted butter
Corn meal

Mix ingredients together. Add enough corn meal to make thick batter. Spread upon buttered tin. Bake 40 minutes. Baste several times with pastry stick dipped in melted butter. Break apart to eat. Johnny Cake is a corruption of Journey Cake, originally used on long journeys.

Sour Milk Waffles

1½ cups flour
3 teaspoons baking powder
¼ teaspoon soda
½ teaspoon salt
2 teaspoons sugar
1 cup sour milk
2 egg yolks, well beaten
4 tablespoons melted butter
2 egg whites, beaten stiff

Mix and sift dry ingredients. Add sour milk gradually, egg yolks, butter, and egg whites. Cook on hot griddle. Serve with maple syrup. Makes 8-12 waffles.

Blueberry Pancakes

3 eggs
1 cup sifted flour
3 teaspoons baking powder
½ teaspoon salt
2 teaspoons sugar
1 teaspoon light brown sugar
½ cup buttermilk
2 tablespoons melted butter
1 package frozen blueberries, thawed, or
   1¼ cups fresh blueberries

In large bowl of electric mixer, at high speed, beat eggs until light and fluffy, about 2 minutes. Into eggs sift flour with baking powder, salt and white sugar. Add the light brown sugar, and beat until smooth.

Stir in buttermilk and butter just until combined. Do not overbeat. Gently stir in berries, being careful not to break them.

Meanwhile, heat griddle or heavy skillet. Use ¼ cup batter for each pancake. Cook until bubbles form on surface and edges become dry. Turn, cook 2 minutes or until nicely browned on underside. Serve with whipped butter and sour cream topping. Makes 12 pancakes.

Blueberry Muffins

2 cups sifted flour
3 teaspoons baking powder
3 tablespoons sugar
Salt
Milk
1 egg, well beaten
½ cup melted butter
1 cup blueberries

Sift flour and measure. Combine with baking powder, sugar, salt. Sift again. Combine milk and beaten egg; mix with dry ingredients. Add butter; mix until flour is dampened. Fold in blueberries, fill buttered muffin tins ⅔ full, and bake at 400° for 25 minutes. Makes 12.

Doughnuts

3½ cups sifted flour
4½ teaspoons baking powder
½ teaspoon cinnamon
½ teaspoon nutmeg
1 teaspoon salt
3 tablespoons shortening
1 cup granulated sugar
2 eggs, well beaten
1 cup milk
About ½ cup sifted flour

Sift together first 5 ingredients. Cream

44

shortening; gradually add sugar, continuing to mix until light. Add eggs; beat well. Add flour mixture alternately with milk, mixing well after each addition.

Add enough of ½ cup flour to make soft, easily handled dough. Chill 1 hour or longer. On floured board, roll dough to ½ inch thickness; cut with floured doughnut cutter. Fry doughnuts in deep fat at 370° until golden brown.

Buttermilk Griddlecakes

1 cup buttermilk
½ cup sweet milk
1 egg, well beaten
1 teaspoon soda
½ teaspoon salt
2 tablespoons melted butter
2 tablespoons corn meal
2 cups flour

Mix ingredients in order given. Heat griddle or frying pan. Grease lightly. Drop mixture from tip of spoon onto griddle. Cook on one side. When puffed, full of bubbles, and cooked at the edges, turn and cook the other side.

Serve with butter, maple syrup, or fruit jams or conserves. Serves 4-6.

Desserts, Conserves

Pumpkin Pie

1¼ cups pumpkin, cooked and strained
⅔ cup sugar
½ teaspoon salt
½ teaspoon ginger
1 teaspoon cinnamon
¼ teaspoon nutmeg
3 eggs, separated
1¼ cups scalded milk
1 six-ounce can (¾ cup) evaporated milk
½ recipe pastry

Thoroughly combine pumpkin, sugar, salt, and spices. Add egg yolks, milk, and blend. Fold in beaten egg whites. Pour into 9-inch pastry-lined pie pan. Bake in 450° oven 10 minutes, then in 325° oven about 45 minutes, or until mixture does not stick to knife. Top with whipped cream if desired. Serves 6.

Apple Pie

3 pounds tart green apples
1 cup sugar
2 tablespoons flour
1/8 teaspoon salt
1 teaspoon cinnamon
1/4 teaspoon nutmeg
1 recipe pastry
4 tablespoons butter

Peel apples and slice thin; add sugar mixed with flour, salt, and spices; fill 9-inch pastry-lined pie pan. Dot with butter. Adjust top crust. Bake in 450° oven 10 minutes, then in 350° oven about 40 minutes. Serves 6.

Apple Cranberry Pie

2 cups cranberries
1 3/4 cups sliced apples
1 1/4 cups sugar
3 tablespoons quick-cooking tapioca
3 tablespoons water
1 recipe pastry

Combine cranberries, apples, sugar, tapioca, and water; let stand so that juices are drawn out. Pour into 9-inch pastry-lined pie pan. Adjust top crust. Bake in 400° oven about 1 hour, or until apples are tender.

Deep Dish Apple Pie

Use ingredients as listed in recipe for Apple Pie, with the exception of pastry. Only ½ recipe pastry is needed. Arrange apples and seasonings in a deep baking pan, or in deep individual baking dishes, cover with pie crust and bake till apples are tender and crust is brown.

Apple Pandowdy

½ cup corn syrup
¼ teaspoon cloves
1 tablespoon cinnamon
¼ teaspoon allspice
5 pounds cooking apples
2 tablespoons butter
¼ teaspoon nutmeg
½ recipe pastry
Sweet cream

Mix corn syrup with spices. Peel and slice apples to fill 3-quart glass baking dish. Dot apples with butter. Pour over them spice mixture. Cover with thick plain pastry.

Bake for 1 hour at 350°. Remove. Cut pastry in squares. Allow to cool. Serve with thick cream. Serves 8.

Cherry Pie

½ cup cherry juice
2 tablespoons sugar
1 tablespoon quick-cooking tapioca
⅛ teaspoon salt
2 tablespoons butter
2 cups pitted cherries
1 recipe pastry

Combine juice, sugar, tapioca, and salt; cook until thick; add some butter and pour over cherries in 8-inch pastry-lined pie pan. Dot with butter. Lay on top crust. Bake about 40 minutes.

Indian Pudding

2 cups scalded milk
⅓ cup corn meal
2 cups cold milk
½ cup molasses
1 teaspoon salt
¼ cup sugar
¼ cup butter
1 teaspoon ginger
  or cinnamon
½ cup raisins, optional
Sweet cream

Pour scalded milk slowly on corn meal, cook in double boiler 20 minutes, add molasses, salt, and ginger. Pour into buttered pudding dish, pour over cold milk, set in pan of hot water, and bake 3 hours in 250° oven. If desired, add raisins to the pudding. Serve with cream.

Blueberry Cake

1/4 pound butter
1 cup sugar
2 eggs, separated
1 1/2 cups flour
1 teaspoon baking powder
1/4 teaspoon salt
1/3 cup milk
1 teaspoon vanilla
1 1/2 cups blueberries

Cream butter, add sugar, and blend together. Beat yolks of eggs well and add to first mixture. Sift flour, baking powder and salt together and add alternately with the milk. Then fold in the stiffly beaten egg whites and vanilla.

Pour half of the batter into a well-greased oblong pan, cover with the blueberries and then with the remaining batter. Bake in a 350° oven for 35 minutes. Sprinkle with powdered sugar. Serve hot. Serves 8 generously.

Mince Tarts

1 pound suet, finely chopped
1 pound currants
1 pound seedless raisins
½ pound white raisins
1 pound apples, chopped
¼ pound mixed candied citron
1 pound superfine sugar
¼ cup Brandy
½ teaspoon each, mace, nutmeg, cinnamon
Juice ½ lemon
Prepared pastry

Mix all ingredients together, press into jars, cover tightly. Keep in cool dry place for 3 or 4 weeks before using. This makes 4-5 pounds of mincemeat.

Tarts: Using a cookie cutter, cut 24 circles from prepared pastry dough. Line the 12 holes of a patty pan or muffin pan. Prick bottom of each tart with a fork to prevent rising. Put in 2 heaping teaspoons of mincemeat. Cover with remaining circles, pinching around the edge to hold together. Bake. Serve hot, dredged with fine sugar. Makes 12.

Mince pies can also be made from this recipe, and are great favorites in New England for Thanksgiving or Christmas dinners.

Shortcake

2 cups flour
1/4 cup sugar
4 teaspoons baking powder
1/2 teaspoon salt
1/2 cup butter
1 egg, well beaten
1/8 cup milk

Mix dry ingredients and then sift; work in butter with fork or finger tips, and add egg and milk.

Bake on buttered cookie sheet for 12 minutes in a 450° oven. Serves 8.

Brown Betty

2 cups bread crumbs
1/4 cup softened butter
4 cups sour apples, sliced
1/3 cup brown sugar
1/4 teaspoon nutmeg, grated
1/2 teaspoon cinnamon
Juice and grated rind of 1/2 lemon
1/2 cup hot water

First mix crumbs and butter lightly with fork. Cover bottom of buttered glass baking dish with crumbs and spread over half the apples, sprinkle with half the sugar, nutmeg, cinnamon, lemon juice, and rind mixed together; repeat. Cover with remaining crumbs and water, and bake 40 minutes in 350° oven. Serve with cream. Serves 6.

Molasses Cookies

2¼ cups sifted flour
1 teaspoon ginger
1 teaspoon cinnamon
¼ teaspoon salt
2 teaspoons baking soda
2 tablespoons hot water
½ cup soft butter
½ cup sugar
½ cup molasses
1 egg
6 tablespoons cold water
½ cup seedless raisins

Sift together first 4 ingredients. Dissolve soda in hot water. Mix butter and next 3 ingredients until creamy; mix in flour mixture alternately with cold water; then mix in soda and all but a few raisins. Drop by tablespoonsful, 2 inches apart, onto greased cookie sheet. Sprinkle with remaining raisins. Bake in 400° oven 12 minutes. Yields 2 dozen.

If smaller cookies are desired drop dough by teaspoonsful.

Old-Fashioned Rice Pudding

⅓ cup uncooked rice
2 cups milk
2 eggs
2 tablespoons butter
¾ cup brown sugar, firmly packed
½ cup raisins
½ teaspoon vanilla
Heavy cream

Wash rice thoroughly, drain and pour into top of a double boiler with milk, and cook over boiling water, stirring frequently for 1 hour. Just before rice is done, separate eggs and beat yolks slightly.

At end of the hour, take rice off the stove and stir in the butter. Then gradually stir in the beaten yolks, stirring constantly so as not to curdle the eggs.

Add brown sugar and raisins to the rice mixture along with the vanilla extract. Set mixture aside and allow to cool.

Start your oven at 325°. While rice mixture is cooling beat up the egg whites until stiff enough to stand in peaks, then fold into the cooled rice. Pour into a medium-size greased casserole, place in a pan of hot water and bake 30 minutes. Serve with heavy cream. Serves 6.

Cape Cod Oatmeal Cookies

1 egg
1 cup sugar
1 cup melted butter
1 tablespoon molasses
1 teaspoon soda
1 teaspoon cinnamon
2½ cups rolled oats
½ cup raisins or ½ cup walnuts
2 cups flour

Beat egg slightly, add other ingredients. Mix well. Drop by spoonsful on buttered cookie sheet. Press flat with fingers. Bake in 325° oven for 15 minutes.

Sugar Cookies

½ cup soft butter
½ cup sugar
1 egg
1 tablespoon milk or cream
½ teaspoon vanilla
½ teaspoon lemon extract
1½ cups flour
1 teaspoon cream of tartar
½ teaspoon soda
¼ teaspoon salt

Combine ingredients in above order. Chill dough. Roll out very thin, about

1/16 of an inch. Cut into fancy shapes with cookie cutters — sprinkle with colored sugar and bake at 400° on greased cookie sheets until very lightly browned — about 5-6 minutes. Watch carefully to keep from over-browning. One recipe makes about 80 small cookies.

Gingerbread

½ cup shortening
½ cup sugar
1 egg
2½ cups flour
1½ teaspoons cinnamon
1 teaspoon baking soda
1 teaspoon ginger
½ teaspoon cloves
½ teaspoon salt
1 cup molasses
1 cup hot water
½ pint heavy cream

Cream together shortening and sugar. Add egg and beat well. Sift together all remaining ingredients. Mix molasses and water together. Add alternately with flour mixture to creamed mixture.

Bake in 350° oven 40 minutes, in a greased 8 x 8 pan. Top with whipped cream.

Ginger Cookies

½ cup shortening
½ cup sugar
½ cup light molasses
½ tablespoon vinegar
1 egg, beaten
3 cups flour
¼ teaspoon salt
½ teaspoon soda
½ teaspoon cinnamon
½ teaspoon ginger

Bring shortening, sugar, molasses, and vinegar to a boil. Cool and add egg. Add sifted dry ingredients; mix well. Chill. Roll on lightly floured surface. Cut any desired shape. Bake on greased cookie sheet in 375° oven 12 to 15 minutes. Makes 30 cookies. Use this recipe also for gingerbread men.

Rhubarb Conserve

4 pounds rhubarb
5 pounds sugar
1 pound seeded raisins
1 lemon, rind and juice
3 oranges, cut in small pieces

Clean stalks of rhubarb and cut in 1-inch pieces. Put in kettle, sprinkle with sugar, and add raisins, grated rind and juice of lemon and pieces of orange. Mix, cover, and let stand ½ hour. Place on range, bring to boiling point, and let simmer 45 minutes, stirring almost constantly. Fill jelly glasses with mixture, cool, and seal with paraffin.

Watermelon Rind

Watermelon rind
1 teaspoon slacked lime
½ cup vinegar
1 cup sugar
1 teaspoon mace
1 teaspoon cinnamon
1 teaspoon ginger
¼ pound raisins

Remove the green outer rind, and pink watermelon. Use only the white rind. Cut into slices. Place in a kettle of water, add a teaspoon of slacked lime and let stand overnight, or for 10 to 12 hours.

Prepare a syrup of vinegar, sugar, mace, cinnamon, ginger and raisins. Wash rind slices. Add syrup. Cook until clear and tender. When done, pour rind into sterilized jars, and seal when cool.

Spiced Crab Apples

10 pounds crab apples
10 cups sugar
Whole cloves

Wash apples, leaving on the stems. Place 10 cups granulated sugar and an equal quantity of water in a large kettle and boil until syrupy. Add crab apples into which have been stuck 2 whole cloves per apple and simmer gently until apples are tender. Turn the apples out into glass jars, cover with syrup and let stand until cool. Cap jars when thoroughly cold.

Ginger Pears

10 pounds ripe pears
5 pounds sugar
¼ pound preserved ginger
5 lemons

Wash pears and remove stems. Core and pare. Cut in small pieces. Add sugar and ginger; let stand overnight. Cut lemon in small pieces; remove seeds. Add lemon to pear mixture. Bring to boiling point; boil slowly, stirring occasionally, 3 hours or until thick. Pour into hot, sterilized jars, filling to top. Fasten covers at once.

Cranberry Conserve

4 cups cranberries
⅔ cup cold water
⅔ cup boiling water
1 cup seeded raisins
1 orange, cut in small pieces
1½ pounds sugar
1 cup walnuts, chopped

Wash and clean cranberries. Add cold water and boil until the skins break. Force through a strainer and add boiling water, seeded raisins, orange, which has been cut in small pieces, and sugar.

Again bring to boiling point and simmer 20 minutes. Add nut meats, chopped coarsely. Cool, fill glasses and seal with paraffin.

Cranberry Mold

4 cups cranberries
2 cups boiling water
3 cups sugar
Orange rind, grated

Pour boiling water over cranberries and cook about 15 minutes. Add sugar and rind and cook 5 minutes. Mold. Serves 8.